MW00979661

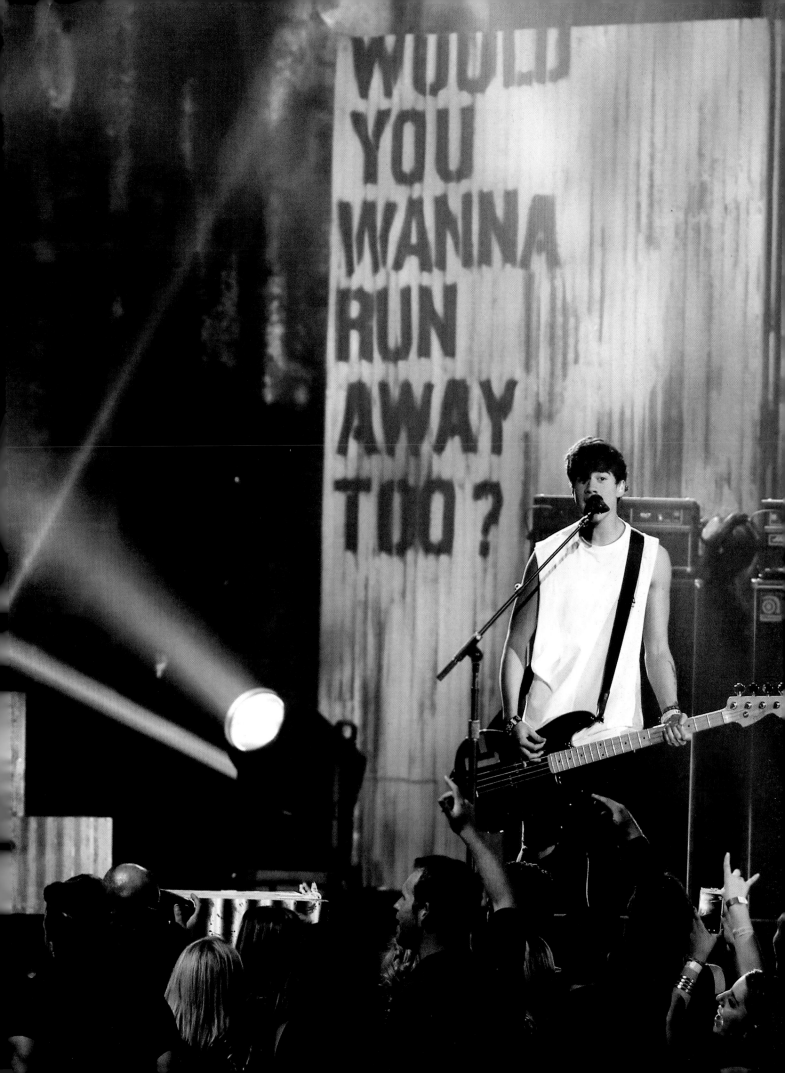

Contents

Text by Ernesto Assante

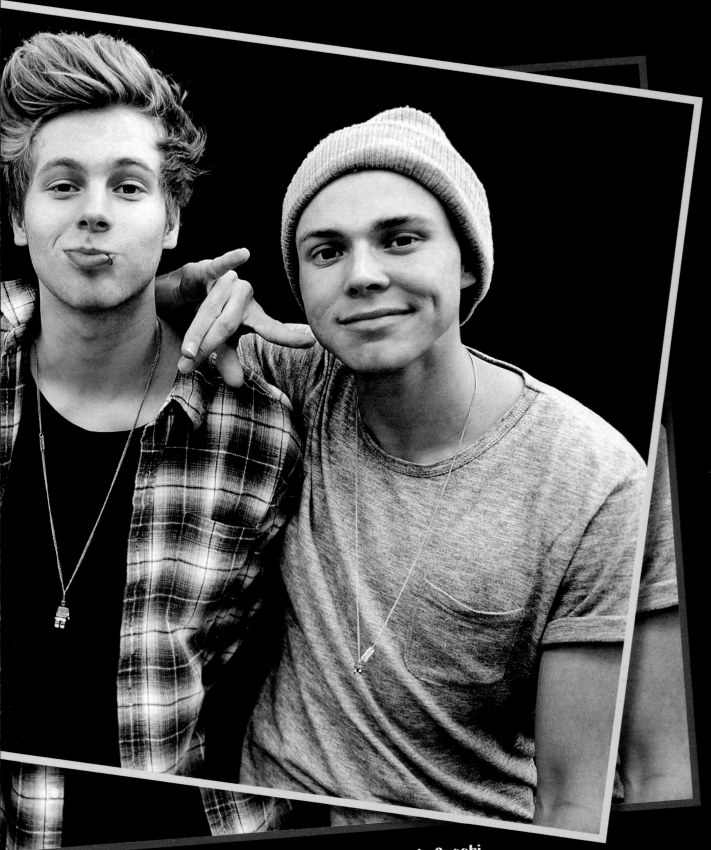

Graphic design Maria Cucchi

Love at first sight

Take four cute, likable boys from Sydney.

Add a heavy dose of rock,

the fast, electric and fun kind,

enhanced by powerful melodies

that lend themselves to harmonies.

What you get is some idea of what lies

behind 5 SECONDS OF SUMMER,

the highest-profile band of the moment.

Luke Hemmings, Calum Hood, Michael Clifford and Ashton Irwin are four young rockers

who love music, girls and having fun. However, they also want to grow,

become musicians and write songs that will be around for a lot longer than just

"5 seconds of summer". This extraordinary phenomenon

has fans going crazy all over the world.

To understand, exactly, who they are, all you need do is see them live and listen to their songs. You'll be swept away by their music and their happy-go-lucky attitude, something that's already happened to hundreds of thousands of fans all over the world, in just a few months. This book tells the story of how one album, a handful of singles, and two tours with One Direction have transformed Ashton, Luke, Calum and Michael into a successful band, four friends ready to take over the world with their energy.

Norwest Christian College is a private school on the

outskirts of Sydney, Australia. Like so many other schools, it has

large classrooms, a gym, sports fields, stadiums, and laboratories. In other words,

it's a good place to get an education. Perhaps too good for students like Calum Hood and

Michael Clifford. They were mad about music, rock and pop songs. They liked to dream about music.

In truth, they attended school, studied, and even did their homework. But, all the while, their

thoughts revolved around forming a band. Yet, they were only two people, and not many others in

the school shared their dream. In fact, because of their love of music, the other students thought that

Calum and Michael were a little strange. But, when Calum met Luke Hemmings, during the school's

open day, things changed. He realized, immediately, that Luke was a kindred spirit and would make an

excellent band member; he was sharp, on the ball, and very likeable. Michael, however, did not agree;

on the contrary, he **and Luke didn't hit it off** at first. However, they had music in common, and little by little their mutual mistrust faded away, and they became **very close friends**, which transformed the trio into a real band. Luke was the one who encouraged and stimulated the others; he was the one **who posted** their first performances **on YouTube**. The three began to play covers, in December 2011.

They uploaded some videos to YouTube, partly for fun and partly to fulfill their dream of imitating leading bands with their videos and receiving millions of hits. On Luke's YouTube channel, they posted a cover of Mike Posner's *Please Don't Go* and their schoolmates immediately realized that those 'strange' boys were not so bad after all. Their ploy worked, viewers liked their music and the three continued to perform covers on YouTube, where they became extremely popular, almost overnight. Then, Calum, Michael and Luke realized that the videos were not enough. They wanted to organize a real concert, perform for their friends, and test their mettle with a live show. But there was a problem: something was missing. Calum played bass guitar, and Michael and Luke guitar, and all three did vocals. But there was no rhythm, no pulse: they needed a drummer. Step forward Ashton Irwin, who, at 17, was handsome and sure of himself. In truth, he didn't particularly like the other three at first; he thought they were cocky, rowdy muddlers. He had seen them online and they did not totally convince him. Yet, the chance to be able to play in front of a large, live audience, in front of hundreds of students, led him to try out for the band. He went to Luke's house, where the band members were waiting to audition him. Ashton found it difficult to socialize with the others; he didn't even play video games. But, when he sat behind his drums, the others knew that they had the drummer they needed, and were now a real band, a rock band.

All four loved rock, the rapid, electric sound of pop-punk bands, especially Blink-182, as well as the Ramones. For them, this was music that entertained people, played with high energy and enthusiasm, music in which boredom was taboo, with singalong melodies and compelling rhythms. The formula worked, the four young men had ideas and played continuously, while their fanbase on the social networks grew considerably. In fact, the band had so many fans that they attracted the attention of some leading publishers and labels. They signed their first contract with Sony/ATV and, a short time later, released their first EP,

Unplugged, which soon reached number 3 in the Australian iTunes chart, **as well as gaining** an **international following**. The band worked hard, wrote prodigiously and also found two fundamental partners, **Christian Lo Russo** and **Joel Chapman**, with whom they improved their sound and developed their compositions, producing new songs.

5SOS came to the attention not only of the general public – who loved their music, their look and their energy – but also of a certain Louis Tomlinson, a young man who was a member of One Direction. Tomlinson saw the band's YouTube video of *Gotta Get Out* and tweeted his link to their video clip. But that was not all. Niall Horan, another member of One Direction, did the

same thing, posting the link of the video clip of the first official 5SOS single, *Out of My Limit*. That was in November 2012, marking the beginning of an extraordinary and incredible adventure for the four boys from Sydney. The *Out of My Limits* video was seen more than 100,000 times in the first 24 hours, the band's fame increased at an exponential rate, and in a short time, the label decided to bet on them and their future. This was not an ordinary boy band. All four members could play and sing, they knew how to write songs, they obviously loved rock and, what was more, were very much admired by the fans of One Direction and by those who follow pop, because their formula was simple, immediate, captivating and fun. Then there was the fact that they were handsome, likeable boys, perfect for a generation that was looking for young men to fall in love with.

In December 2012, the band went to the UK to work with some of the best English musicians. They met McFly, worked with Roy Stride of Scouting for Girls, Nick Hodgson of the Kaiser Chiefs, James Bourne of Busted and Jamie Scott, all of whom were musicians who knew pop and rock inside out and were more than willing to help the young Aussies to hone their songwriting skills and develop their ideas and passions, in order make the 5SOS sound and songs original and powerful. Once again, it was One Direction that put them on the right track, so to speak, by choosing them as the support band for their Take Me Home tour, which began at the O2 Arena in London toward the beginning of 2013.

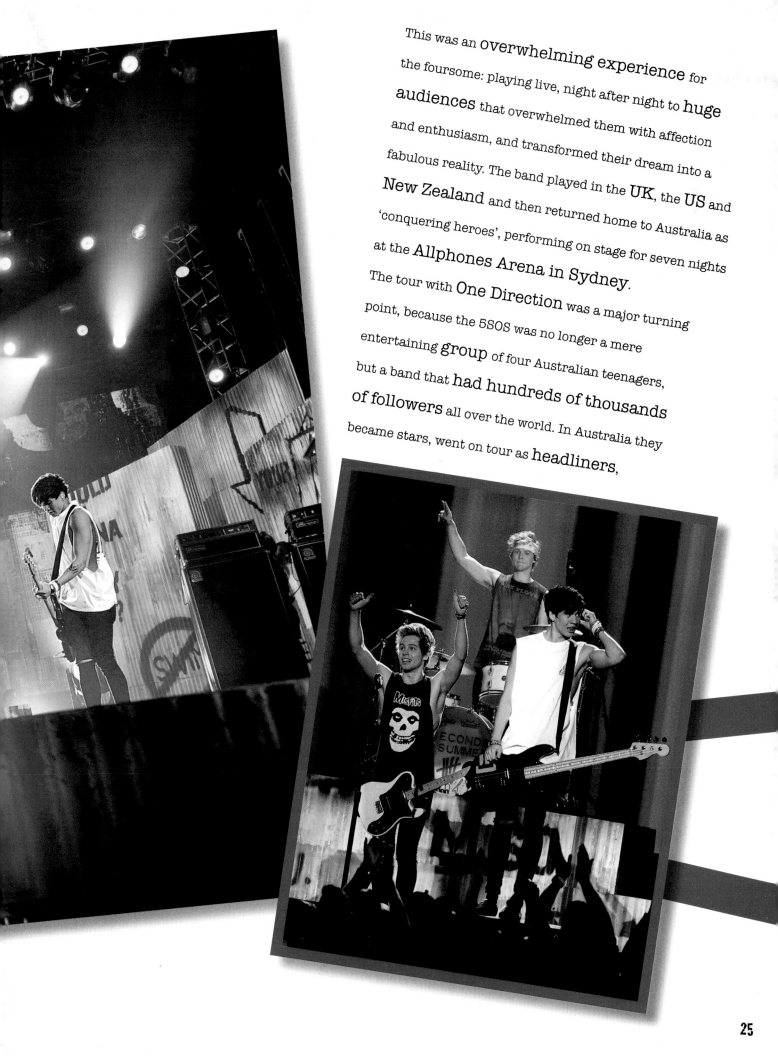

This was an overwhelming experience for the foursome: playing live, night after night to huge audiences that overwhelmed them with affection and enthusiasm, and transformed their dream into a fabulous reality. The band played in the UK, the US and New Zealand and then returned home to Australia as 'conquering heroes', performing on stage for seven nights at the Allphones Arena in Sydney. The tour with One Direction was a major turning point, because the 5SOS was no longer a mere entertaining group of four Australian teenagers, but a band that had hundreds of thousands of followers all over the world. In Australia they became stars, went on tour as headliners,

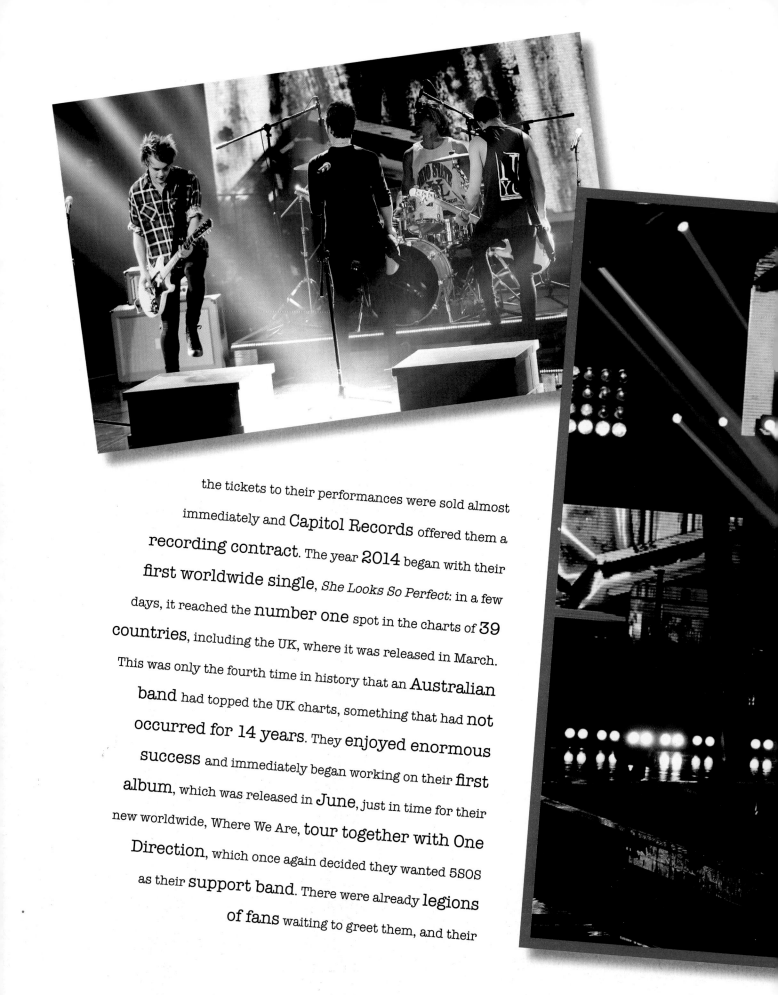

the tickets to their performances were sold almost immediately and Capitol Records offered them a recording contract. The year 2014 began with their first worldwide single, *She Looks So Perfect*: in a few days, it reached the number one spot in the charts of 39 countries, including the UK, where it was released in March. This was only the fourth time in history that an Australian band had topped the UK charts, something that had not occurred for 14 years. They enjoyed enormous success and immediately began working on their first album, which was released in June, just in time for their new worldwide, Where We Are, tour together with One Direction, which once again decided they wanted 5SOS as their support band. There were already legions of fans waiting to greet them, and their concerts were a nothing short of a triumph. They worked hard to create their album: in a year they wrote almost 100 songs and, with that incredible portfolio, they went in to the recording studio, with the aid of experienced and qualified people like Alex Gaskarth of All Time Low, one of the Australia's favorite bands, the Madden Brothers, and songwriters like John Feldmann, Jake Sinclair and Steve Robson – all ready and willing to create the best pop rock album in circulation.

The band's sound was dominated by guitars, just like every self-respecting rock band, but the spirit was pop, which was perfect music for a large party, such as the ones they proposed during their live performances. "We like our shows to be big party vibes, y'know?" Luke says. "We want a show the fans can get involved in." They have been influenced by many bands, many of which played music from different genres. Besides All Time Low, which all four like and respect, two of their main influences were the pop-punk bands Green Day and Blink-182, Ashton stated, but another big favorite was Paramore and, more recently, Arctic Monkeys and Imagine Dragons. He also said that 5SOS did not want to be a band that was famous for a couple of years only to disappear. "We just want to be the biggest and the best band that we can be really, see how far we can take it." They also like bands like Good Charlotte and Yellowcard, and they want to take that kind of sound and modernize it. Another of their pursuits is to make bands become fashionable again.

Calum

given name **Calum Thomas**

family name **Hood**

date of birth **25 January 1996**

color of hair **dark brown**

color of eyes **dark brown**

instrument **bass guitar**

Calum Thomas Hood was born on 25 January 1996. His zodiac sign is **Aquarius**, and, like all self-respecting Aquarians, he is **creative**, a **dreamer, a libertarian,** and **optimistic** and music means everything to him. But, the truth is that music was not Calum's first calling. As a youngster, **he loved to play soccer** and dreamt of playing for a major team, practicing hard three times a week. Then, **one day, he discovered the bass guitar** and began to play with his pal Michael, at first just a few times a week and then more and more frequently, until he abandoned soccer for his true vocation.

Calum is a **prolific songwriter**, beginning a new one as soon as finishes the preceding one. Like the other members of the band, **he loves rock, as well as pop**, the songs of Destiny's Child and Beyoncé, and the look of Katy Perry, with whom he would like to be stuck in an elevator for a few hours.

never go out with a girl under 14, and **prefers those who love music** as much as he does. Calum **is a real nerd** and is proud of it. Apparently, he used **not to like 'cool'** people but has started to appreciate them; he is also convinced that his fans think he is 'cooler' than he really is. Calum has simple tastes when it comes to cuisine, an exception being ham and **pineapple pizza**. He is **very close to his family**, especially his sister; in fact, he became quite emotional during her high school graduation ceremony. He **loves to go to the movies**, adores cartoons, and really likes *The Hunger Games*. Despite the fact that he is very athletic, **he has never learned to skateboard. He is passionate about videogames,** loves IT, and is **a geek in the recording studio** as he looks for new sounds for the band. His smartphone is always on and he is the first one who answers calls from the band's friends because **he is always, always,** there for his friends and is the friend everyone would like to have. It's difficult to argue with him because **nastiness and envy are not in his DNA.** He is a dreamer and, like Michael, left school before graduation in order to develop his love for Rock'n'Roll and music in general. **He and Michael were founders of the band,** the ones who were first to decide that music was, and would always be, the linchpin of their lives. His motto is "be yourself, even if, to other people, this doesn't seem to be enough."

Michael

Michael Gordon Clifford has a difficult character. Firstly, **he doesn't like his middle name, Gordon,** and never uses it. Secondly, he **doesn't like the color of his hair,** to such a degree that he doesn't even remember what it is (it is light brown, by the way). In fact, Michael's **hair may have a different color every day,** depending on his mood. And, it is not necessarily all the same color, but also has original combinations that he creates himself. And, as if that were not enough, he **doesn't even like his signature and so changes it continuously,** leaving his fans (especially the girls) perplexed at the different autographs he gives them. **School and studies** are not exactly his favorite sport. He **prefers videogames,** which he can play for a whole day. Better yet, he likes to laze around on the sofa or lie in bed as much as possible. But this does not mean that he is not a lively boy. In fact, Michael **is the 'craziest' member of 5SOS,** always ready to joke and prank and to go out with his friends to a noisy party until the small hours.

given name	Michael Gordon
family name	Clifford
date of birth	20 November 1996
color of hair	"variable"
color of eyes	green
instrument	guitar

Michael did not have an easy childhood. He was raised by his mother, Karen, and has never met his father. "The 5SOS fans are the only family I ever had," he now states, but for many years, his best friend has been his guitar, an Epiphone Les Paul, his first guitar, with which he learned the songs of his favorite rock bands (he loves All Time Low), and also wrote his own songs. Michael is a happy person and still likes to play, especially with dolls or with My Little Pony. He was the one who 'invented' the name of the band, which came to him during a math lesson in school. The other members of the band don't particularly like the name itself, but they think the initials, 5SOS, are fantastic. He loves Italian food but is certainly not one of those people who likes to share their portions with others. What is certain is that he wants to be a superhero and that changing the color of his hair continuously is the source of his extraordinary gifts or 'super powers', especially his guitar playing. He uses these powers, above all, to attract girls, whom he adores, always trying to make them laugh.

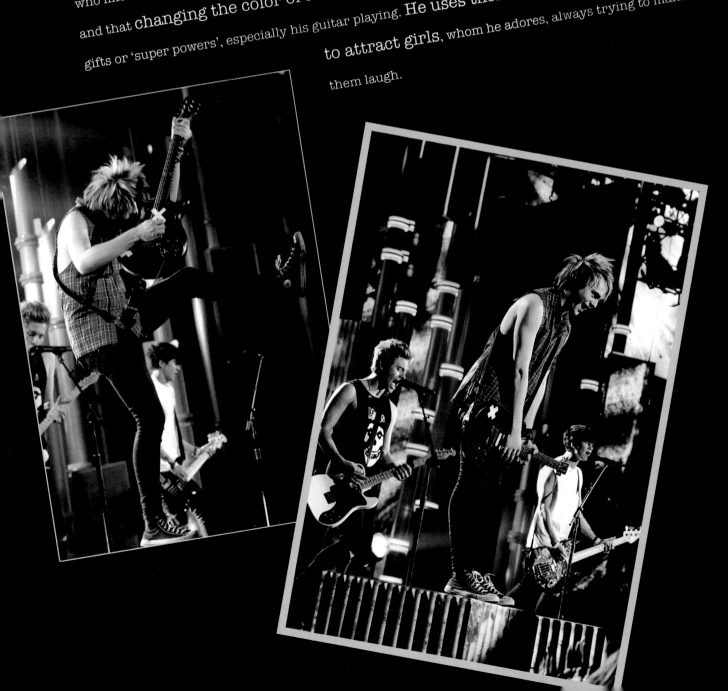

Luke

If 5SOS exists at all, it is thanks to Luke Hemmings. He was the one who opened a channel on YouTube, in 2011, where he uploaded videos of himself singing covers of famous singers. And, when he, Michael and Calum formed the band, they posted their first videos on that same channel, becoming well known almost overnight. Luke, who was born in Sydney on 16 July 1996, has always loved technology – computers, smartphones, videogames (Super Mario Kart is his favorite). This certainly has not stopped him from becoming quite adept at the snowboard, from cruising along the streets on his skateboard or from playing soccer.

given name	Luke
family name	Hemmings
date of birth	16 July 1996
color of hair	blond
color of eyes	light blue
instrument	guitar

In other words, he enjoys 'going on a rampage' on his own, whenever there is an opportunity to do so, which, however, should not give us the impression that he does not have a good home life. On the contrary, he has a very close relationship with his family. His mother, Liz, his father, Andrew, and his brothers Ben and Jack have always supported Luke's passion for music, especially rock, despite the noise coming from his room at all hours of the day and night. He has a dog, Molly, loves to eat (he is curious about all kinds of food and is willing to try them all, but he simply adores pizza, frozen yogurt, ham and cheese and especially a spread called Vegemite. However, his favorite food is ice cream: he once won a contest at Pizza Hut by eating 17 cups of ice cream. He is a very meticulous young man, and others say he is the most responsible member of the band, the one who makes sure everything is ready before every concert.

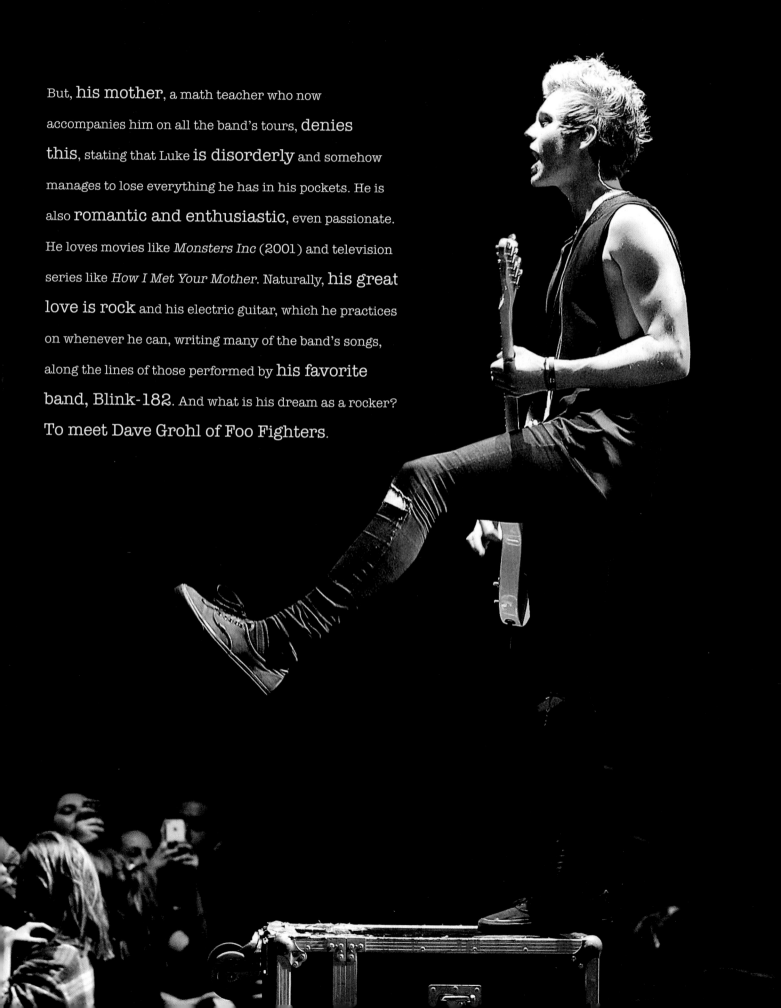

But, his mother, a math teacher who now accompanies him on all the band's tours, denies this, stating that Luke is disorderly and somehow manages to lose everything he has in his pockets. He is also romantic and enthusiastic, even passionate. He loves movies like *Monsters Inc* (2001) and television series like *How I Met Your Mother*. Naturally, his great love is rock and his electric guitar, which he practices on whenever he can, writing many of the band's songs, along the lines of those performed by his favorite band, Blink-182. And what is his dream as a rocker? To meet Dave Grohl of Foo Fighters.

Ashton

given name	Ashton Fletcher
family name	Irwin
date of birth	7 July 1994
color of hair	blond
color of eyes	brownish green
instrument	drums

Ashton Fletcher Irwin, at just 20, is the 'old man' of the band. He was born on 7 July 1994 and his astrological sign is Cancer. He loves sports, especially swimming and ice skating, and has an athletic physique. But he uses all his energy to play his drums. In fact, this is what he loves most in life, so much so that his fondest childhood memory, when he was eight years old, was the first time he played the drums for a few members of his family. Music is his passion. Besides the drums, he plays saxophone, guitar and piano, and, like other band members, he writes songs and takes part in other creative pursuits. He could not live without music, and, were he not performing live and recording with the band, he would certainly be teaching music to youngsters. Ashton's parents are separated but he has a good relationship with both of them, and he is especially attached to his younger brothers Harry and Lauren. Yet he is an independent young man. Before joining the band, he attended school (his favorite subject was art) while working in a fast food restaurant so that he could be his own man. Ashton is the only member of the band who has a history in another band, Swallow the Goldfish, a name inspired by the movie A Fish Called Wanda (1988).

Pop and punk are his favorite music genres, and he is able to combine the songs of James Morrison, Paramore, Coldplay and Green Day, light but electrifying melodies, and rock and standard songs – all of which he does by singing while playing his drums at a furious pace. But, he also has a lot of fun with One Direction. He knows how to cook and enjoys doing this for the band, especially spaghetti, his favorite dish. He also likes to try out new recipes, forcing his colleagues to taste his creations. His mother says he has always been a responsible, happy and affectionate boy, and the other band members appreciate his ability to listen to and try to understand others.

He is **very romantic**, but can't describe his ideal girl, and he firmly believes that life offers you extraordinary opportunities to demonstrate what you are capable of achieving. In fact, his favorite movie is Gabriele Muccino's *The Pursuit of Happyness* (2006). **He hates sleeping alone** and is still afraid of the dark.

Ernesto Assante, is a correspondent for Italy's "La Repubblica" newspaper, music critic, author and TV and radio host. Alongside Gino Castaldo, he presents "Playlist" on Radio Capital and "Webnotte" on Repubblica.tv. He has written several books, including "Legends of Rock" for White Star Publishers (2007) and "Beatles" with Gino Castaldo for Laterza (2014).

Photographic Credits

WHITE STAR PUBLISHERS

WS White Star Publishers' is a registered trademark property of De Agostini Libri S.p.A.

© 2014 De Agostini Libri S.p.A.
Via G. da Verrazano, 15
28100 Novara, Italy
www.whitestar.it - www.deagostini.it

Translation: Richard Pierce
Editing: Norman Gilligan

ISBN 978-88-544-0932-3
1 2 3 4 5 6   18 17 16 15 14

Printed in Italy